MONEY TALK

Managing My Life—God's Way

Pastor Mark Jeske

Published by Straight Talk Books
P.O. Box 301, Milwaukee, WI 53201
800.661.3311 • timeofgrace.org

Printed in the United States of America
ISBN: 978-1-942107-01-9

TIME OF GRACE *and* IT ALL STARTS NOW *are registered marks of Time of Grace Ministry.*

Contents

Introduction..4

The Story of Money..6

God in the Middle..8

Mammon.. 13

Accumulating Wealth... 17

What Holds People Back?... 22

Work... 25

Spending.. 28

How Much Is Enough?..30

Debt... 32

Generosity... 35

Saving and Investing... 39

Cheating... 41

Lending...44

Gambling 46

Taxes...48

Your Financial Legacy... 51

Conclusion... 53

Introduction

Money makes the world go 'round.

It sure does. Back in the 1960s, Joel Gray sang those words with a smirk and a strut in the musical *Cabaret*. Rapper R. Kelly wrote a song with that same title about 30 years later. Money is portable power. It has the remarkable ability to get other people to do things for you. Now digitized, it can fly around the world and back with a few mouse clicks or screen taps. Money gets you attention, adventures, treats, and comfort. Money can be stored; although if it sits still, it slowly loses value each hour because of inflation. It can also be stolen.

Money might be defined as easily convertible financial instruments, like direct holding of dollars. But wealth can be accumulated in many ways—treasury bonds, rare art, gold bullion, real estate, livestock, mutual funds, ownership of a business, copyrights to intellectual property, collectible cars, and virtual funds like Bitcoin.

Money gives people choices—what kind of home they will live in, the kind of car they will drive, how and where they will eat, and where they will travel. Money determines your children's education and the type of nursing home care you will receive. Money brings power, but that power is seductive. Money easily becomes an idol, which Scripture sometimes calls *Mammon.* A family that has a healthy attitude about money will likely be a peaceful one. Sad to say, when there is conflict in a home, the most likely cause of that stress is money dysfunction.

Much of what I know about money can be attributed to my dear parents. I will always be grateful to my father for teaching me the values of God first, hard work, self-discipline, and the dignity of living small. I appreciate my mother's wisdom too—I can still see her sorting out piles of tens, fives, and singles of Dad's monthly paycheck into envelopes tagged for utilities, transportation, food, church offerings, and entertainment. When the entertainment envelope was empty, we made our own fun for the rest of the month.

God's wonderful Word will provide inspiration and guidance for you to grow in money wisdom and generosity.

It is my hope in this short book to dig into the Bible with you for the powerful insights we will find there. God's wonderful Word will provide inspiration and guidance for you to grow in money wisdom and generosity. In this way you and your family will honor God, enjoy greater financial security, and be able to grow in the impact you can have through your charitable contributions.

The Story of Money

Money has taken various forms in human history. Throughout most of the Old Testament, business transactions were based either on livestock; barter of valuable commodities like sheep fleeces; or bullion bars of valuable metals like gold, silver, or bronze. The Jewish *shekel* was originally a weight, and so was the Greek *talenton*, from which our word *talent* is derived (Matthew 25:14-30). Each merchant was expected to produce scales and accurate weights to measure out the pieces of the metal bars. Coinage, i.e., circular pieces of precious metal issued and imprinted by a government, seems to have arisen in Greece and Asia Minor in the seventh and sixth centuries B.C. and quickly spread as a means of financial exchange. Greeks minted *drachmas*, *tetradrachmas*, and *staters*; Persians the *daric*; Syrians the *mina*; and Romans the *denarius*. Even the Jews had their *shekels* and *lepta* (mites).

The precious metals in the coins made them intrinsically valuable; the government that stamped them guaranteed a certain degree of purity. In the U.S., precious metals were formerly used for the bigger coins, but 1964 was the last year our coins had any silver in them. Since that date the metal in a dime, for instance, is worth less than 10 cents, but the silver in the pre-1964 coins gives them a value of two dollars or more. They are steadily being melted down.

Paper money was invented by the Chinese in the seventh century, but banknotes didn't become widespread in Europe until the late 1600s. Today's transactions are becoming more cashless all the time—credit cards, debit cards, gift cards, and even smartphone payment apps are everywhere. A restaurant I worked at in the 1970s refused to take credit cards. Any restaurant foolish enough to try that today wouldn't be in business the second week.

The Bible has a lot to say about money—the word occurs over 110 times, besides many references to wealth, silver, and gold. The book of Proverbs is a particularly rich vein of godly wisdom about achieving financial security. In Scripture there are stories of godly men and women who had nothing, as well as tales of heroes of faith who were very wealthy. And here is one of the Bible's many paradoxes: although money can become an addictive idol, a root of all kinds of evil (1 Timothy 6:10), the Bible says that the Lord blesses his faithful people with prosperity. God likes to give you things, as much as he dares.

The Bible has a lot to say about money.

God in the Middle

A healthy understanding of money must begin with the One who made it all: **"The earth is the Lord's, and everything in it"** (Psalm 24:1). **"Rich and poor have this in common: The Lord is the Maker of them all"** (Proverbs 22:2). God actually believes that everything in the universe really belongs to him: **"Every animal of the forest is mine,"** he says, **"and the cattle on a thousand hills"** (Psalm 50:10). That includes any real estate you may own, any business you may run, your 401(k), your house, vehicles, summer cottage, and money market funds.

You will never be truly and deeply satisfied and happy with your life unless God is in the middle of it.

Seriously! That means that you will never be truly and deeply satisfied and happy with your life unless God is in the middle of it. The universe was made to revolve around him; happy are those who choose to live that way. It aligns them with the universe's design.

Our coming to faith in Jesus Christ changes how we view the world. Instead of trying to control everything in our little sphere, we come to realize that we are really living in God's world. King Solomon forgot that. In his later years, after he had grown stupendously wealthy but also after his many, many wives had begun to turn his heart away from the Lord, he wrote bitterly that his money and "achievements" seemed to have no meaning whatsoever: **"I amassed silver and gold for myself, and the treasure of kings and provinces. . . . I became greater by far than anyone in Jerusalem before me. . . . I denied myself nothing my eyes desired; I refused my heart no pleasure. . . . Yet when I surveyed all that my hands had done and what I had toiled to achieve, everything was meaningless, a chasing after the wind; nothing was gained under the sun"** (Ecclesiastes 2:8–11).

What was missing for this amazing man was to find his true purpose in fitting into God's agenda—all Solomon could think about was himself, only what was "*under* the sun." He forgot that the Creator of all things lives "*above* the sun." No wonder all his achievements and projects were turning to sand in his hands. Apparently he still remembered at least one of the lessons his godly tutors had taught him in his youth: **"Without him** [i.e., God]**, who can eat or find enjoyment?"** (Ecclesiastes 2:25). And then come judgment and eternity. How sad the people who spent their lives amassing only money: **"Wealth is worthless in the day of wrath"** (Proverbs 11:4).

Your greatest treasure is the gospel of Christ.

Your greatest treasure is the gospel of Christ. The blood he shed for you has paid the price to win God's favor toward you, forgiveness of your sins, a thousand earthly blessings, and the promise of a delightful eternity with him in heaven. Beggars like you and me, impoverished and hopeless, were made secure eternally through the impoverishment of our Savior Jesus: **"You know the grace of our Lord Jesus Christ, that though he was rich, yet for your sake he became poor, so that you through his poverty might become rich"** (2 Corinthians 8:9).

Jesus' words to his disciples are timeless reminders to all believers of what matters most in our lives: **"Do not store up for yourselves treasures on earth, where moths and vermin destroy, and where thieves break in and steal. But store up for yourselves treasures in heaven, where moths and vermin do not destroy, and where thieves do not break in and steal. For where your treasure is, there your heart will be also"** (Matthew 6:19-21).

Jesus told a number of parables about how people viewed and used money. Several times he began one of these memorable stories with the scenario of a wealthy nobleman who entrusted his senior employees with significant amounts of capital: **"A man of noble birth went to a distant country to have himself appointed king and then to return. So he called ten of his servants and gave them ten minas. 'Put this money to work,' he said, 'until I come back'"** (Luke 19:12,13). The point is pretty obvious, isn't it? God, wealthy beyond our comprehension, entrusts us with his property, directs us to put that stuff to work *for his agenda*, and trusts us to manage his property well.

Even as he watches us at work with his financial tools, property, and equipment, he is arranging things from above. Moses cautioned the Israelites not to grow smug and unspiritual as they grew more prosperous: **"You may say to yourself, '*My* power and the strength of *my* hands have produced this wealth for me.' But remember the Lord your God, for it is *he* who gives you the ability to produce wealth"** (Deuteronomy 8:17,18).

All good business principles come from him—making your customers more important than you, always acting in their interest, telling the truth, accepting responsibility, having scrupulous honesty, keeping promises, exceeding expectations, striving for excellence, treating employees fairly, showing no favoritism, never taking advantage of those smaller than you. All those traits of good businesses come from God himself: **"The Lord gives wisdom; from his mouth come knowledge and understanding. He holds success in store for the upright"** (Proverbs 2:6,7).

When you are connected to God, you are connected to his resources.

Worriers, take heart! When you are connected to God, you are connected to his resources. The Father guarantees that you will always have enough (as he defines *enough*, of course). Jesus promises all believers: **"Do not worry, saying,**

'What shall we eat?' or 'What shall we drink?' or 'What shall we wear?' For the pagans run after all these things, and your heavenly Father knows that you need them. But seek first his kingdom and his righteousness, and all these things will be given to you as well" (Matthew 6:31-33). **"Trust in the Lord with all your heart and lean not on your own understanding; in all your ways submit to him, and he will make your paths straight"** (Proverbs 3:5,6).

Involve him in your planning. Pray for understanding, clarity of vision, honest self-appraisal, good people judgment, and his blessings. Humble yourself and do the right things, patiently waiting for him to keep his promises in his time. **"Commit to the Lord whatever you do, and he will establish your plans"** (Proverbs 16:3).

Mammon

"Power tends to corrupt," said Lord Acton, eighth baronet of Shropshire. "Great men are almost always bad men." Money is power, pure and simple, and so it should surprise no one that the lust for money corrupts people. It rotted out the soul even of one of Jesus' disciples, though he basked every day in the presence and words of the very Son of God himself. Judas **"was a thief; as keeper of the money bag, he used to help himself to what was put into it"** (John 12:6).

Our culture, like most cultures in world history, is insanely materialistic. Rapper 50 Cent issued the album *Get Rich or Die Tryin'* that sold 872,000 copies *in its first week.* By the end of the year, it had sold over 12 million copies, making it the biggest album in the industry that year. Luxury industries cater to every possible human appetite with seductive messages that acquiring things will make you happy.

Our culture is insanely materialistic.

The Old Testament contains many warnings to believers about the addictive danger of falling in love with money. Among them: **"The greedy bring ruin to their households"** (Proverbs 15:27). **"Those who trust in their riches will fall"** (Proverbs 11:28). **"Whoever loves money never has enough; whoever loves wealth is never satisfied with their income"** (Ecclesiastes 5:10).

In the New Testament, the majority of references to money and wealth are negative. Jesus himself spoke sharply and often about money sickness, perhaps because his persistent enemies, the Pharisees, were so proud of their wealth and social standing. In their worldview, their prosperity demonstrated that they were morally superior to the rest of the herd. For example, Jesus said, **"'No one can serve two masters. Either you will hate the one and love the other, or you will be devoted to the one and despise the other. You cannot serve both God and money** [in Greek *Mammon*].' **The Pharisees, who loved money, heard all this and were sneering at Jesus"** (Luke 16:13,14).

When Jesus sent out his disciples to do some independent evangelism as part of their training program, he wanted them to experience the joy and freedom of traveling light. They would need to trust God and make friends with people to survive. **"Do not get any gold or silver or copper to take with you in your belts—no bag for the journey or extra shirt or sandals or a staff, for the worker is worth his keep"** (Matthew 10:9,10). In the same way, St. Paul chose to work part time in the canvas trade so that it would be clear to his congregation in Corinth that he was not in it for the money. He supported himself so that he could give his ministry away and remove even the slightest suspicion that he was trying to enrich himself at their expense.

Jesus' stories frequently taught the danger

of money love: in the parable of the lost son, a reckless young man squanders his half of the inheritance his father had built up and given him (Luke 15); in the parable of the rich man and Lazarus (Luke 16), we see a man suffering the torments of hell because he had made money his god. **"Watch**

Jesus' stories frequently taught the danger of money love.

out! Be on your guard against all kinds of greed; life does not consist in an abundance of possessions" (Luke 12:15). He described a rich fool who was obsessed with building a bigger and bigger agricultural empire but who had no time for God or other people. **"But God said to him, 'You fool! This very night your life will be demanded from you. Then who will get what you have prepared for yourself?'"** (Luke 12:20).

Jesus told a rich young ruler that his soul was imperiled with money sickness and that the best thing he could do was liquidate everything, give his assets away, and follow Jesus (Luke 18:18-22). Probably his most famous money remark then followed: Jesus looked at him sadly and said, **"How hard it is for the rich to enter the kingdom of God! Indeed, it is easier for a camel to go through the eye of a needle than for someone who is rich to enter the kingdom of God"** (Luke 18:24,25).

Hard, but of course not impossible. Abraham, Isaac, Jacob, Boaz, and King David were all examples of well-to-do believers. It is important to remember that Jesus often spoke in hyperbole, extreme exaggeration, to make a point. The only way his moneyless disciples would be able to complete their preaching tour is if *somebody else's business produced a surplus so they would have money to spare to give to the disciples.* Jesus famously compared himself unfavorably to foxes and birds, both

The more you love money, the less you will love the people in your life.

of which had homes but he didn't (Luke 9:58). However, he was happy to enjoy the hospitality of friends like Mary, Martha, and Lazarus, who did have a financial surplus, who did have a home in Bethany, and who loved to make him and the disciples feel welcome in that home.

Why is the love of money so bad?

- Because there is such a short path from loving money to the sin of pride.

- Because love of money slowly makes money a god, the thing you care about and trust in more than anything else. All idolatry suffocates faith in Jesus Christ.

- Because the more you love money, the less you will love the people in your life.

- Because loving money will make you miserly and cold toward ministries of the Word and charities that relieve human suffering.

Accumulating Wealth

I'll admit it—it took me quite a few years to absorb the Bible's ideas blessing accumulation of wealth. In my younger years, I don't recall ever hearing any money talk in church except stern warnings about materialism and the annual exhortation to give generously to the church on Stewardship Sunday.

There is so much more in Scripture. It is a fascinating paradox that the same Scriptures that hurl God's curses on greed, materialism, covetousness, and love of money also bring the message that God loves to give financial wealth and prosperity to believers. *What?!* No, really. It's like the two tracks needed for a railroad car to move. We need to keep both teachings in mind, for they are both true.

Poverty is everywhere and has always existed. Because of the human brokenness caused by sin, people will always suffer from the cruelty and neglect of others, especially from the people in their own families. Much poverty is also self-inflicted, brought about by people's own selfishness, shortsightedness, and really bad choices. Dropping out of school, getting in the habit of escaping from life's pressures by using drugs or heavy drinking, causing unwed pregnancies, and running with gangs are effective ways of sinking yourself and others into a deep hole.

Regardless of how people fell or jumped or were pushed into a pit, God has compassion for all his creatures, and he sends the strugglers various kinds of support. He also commands those of his children who have their lives together to extend a helping hand: **"Whoever oppresses the poor shows contempt for their Maker, but whoever is kind to the needy honors God"** (Proverbs 14:31). **"It is a sin to despise one's neighbor, but blessed is the one who is kind to the needy"** (Proverbs 14:21).

It's important that the help offered the poor shows respect to them, is a hand up rather than just a quick handout, shows an interest in them as people and not as just a feel-good project, and ideally is part of a plan to help them get on a positive path out of the hole they're in. Congregations are a great environment in which to help people get the resources they need and not enable the behaviors that are destroying them.

But while God has love and compassion for poor people, *that doesn't make poverty a desirable life goal!* Being broke, deep in debt, homeless, or constantly scrambling just to stay alive is no way to live, and it is really hard on your family if you drag them into that kind of life. **"The poor are shunned by all their relatives—how much more do their friends avoid them! Though the poor pursue them with pleading, they are nowhere to be found"** (Proverbs 19:7). **"The poor are shunned even by their neighbors"** (Proverbs 14:20).

It is an honorable life goal to seek to build your family's wealth. In fact, I would put it like this in talking with my own children and young people from the congregation:

- Get as good a job as you can.

- Work as long and hard as you can.

- Make as much money as you can.

- Save and invest as much as you can.

- Borrow as little as you can.

- Pay off your debts as quickly as you can.

- Get promoted as high as you can.

- Give as generously as you can.

To his children who acknowledge him as Creator and who are aware of the dangers of materialism, God does not hesitate to hold out his promises of material prosperity: **"The blessing of the LORD brings *wealth*"** (Proverbs 10:22). **"Humility is the fear of the LORD; its wages are *riches* and honor and life"** (Proverbs 22:4). **"*Prosperity* is the reward of the righteous"** (Proverbs 13:21 NIV84).

The risks of money sickness are real, and there still are proud Pharisees today, but God still encourages us to work hard and build our family's net worth. He built this incredible world not just as an exercise of his divine creativity and power but to *show us* his wonders and glory! He made the Grand Canyon for *you* to look at. He made the Rockies and the Wasatch for *you* to ski on. He made the great rolling waves off Malibu for *you* to surf on, the Appalachians for hiking, lakes for fishing, the Caribbean reefs for snorkeling, and the great north woods for camping. It is worth working and saving so that you can afford to see these places and thrill at the genius and artistry and power of the God you worship.

Financial literacy is learned behavior—nobody is good at it from birth. Pay attention to your parents, and maybe even more to your grandparents. They are survivors of the struggle for survival and know more about people and money than you do. Ask them questions; learn from them; watch what they do (to imitate their smarts, or perhaps to avoid their mistakes). **"A wise son heeds his father's instruction"** (Proverbs 13:1).

Financial literacy is learned behavior—nobody is good at it from birth.

Find a couple financial mentors whom you admire and can trust. They can be unofficial friends, or perhaps you are ready to take the plunge and consult a professional financial advisor: **"The way of fools seems right to them, but the wise listen to advice"** (Proverbs 12:15). **"Walk with the wise and become wise"** (Proverbs 13:20). **"Plans fail for lack of counsel, but with many advisers they succeed"** (Proverbs 15:22).

The final chapter of Proverbs describes an idealized hardworking wife who is a phenomenal asset to her husband and family. She unabashedly seeks to build the family's finances: **"She considers a field and buys it; out of her *earnings*** she plants a vineyard. She sees that her trading is *profitable*. . . . She is clothed with strength and dignity; she can laugh at the days to come. She speaks with wisdom, and faithful instruction is on her tongue" (Proverbs 31:16,18,25,26).

An amazing real-life example of a Proverbs 31 woman is Katherine von Bora, a Saxon nun who left her convent and married Dr. Martin Luther. When the Reformation erupted in central Germany in the 1520s, many monasteries and cloisters emptied out as the monks and nuns were released from their lifetime vows and bolted for freedom. The Elector of Saxony gave Dr. Luther the residence hall of the now-empty Black Cloister in Wittenberg as a gift for him and his new wife. It had housed Augustinian monks who wore black habits (hence the cloister's name).

What the Luthers lived in was a vast, abandoned, tumbledown masonry building. While the good doctor was occupied with his lectures, scholarly research, frenetic literary output, and heavy preaching schedule, Katie oversaw the building repairs; raised hogs, cattle, ducks, and chickens; built and stocked a fishpond; tended an orchard and garden; did the slaughtering; managed the family money; took in renters and served as landlady; and bought another farm in nearby Zühlsdorf. Oh, and also bore Martin Luther six children. What a woman!

I bet there are some Proverbs 31 women in your congregation.

What Holds People Back?

Why do so many people feel financial stress? Why are their credit scores so low? Why are there so many arguments at home? Why are so many homeowners underwater in their mortgages? Why are so many Americans completely unprepared for retirement? Why do people carry such staggering levels of debt?

In coming chapters, we'll take a closer look at some personal finance destroyers like out-of-control spending, inadequate rate of saving, impatience, and unwise borrowing. Some families are victims of accidental injury or major illness and have inadequate insurance to cover these disasters. Some people don't work very hard at saving because they just assume that there will be Social Security or SSI or Title XIX or other government programs to take care of them. In addition to these, here are Scripture's observations on what holds people back from financial security.

Pretending. You can spend money you don't have trying to pretend that you are on a higher economic rung: **"Better to be a nobody and yet have a servant than pretend to be somebody and have no food"** (Proverbs 12:9).

Laziness. Let's face it—a lot of jobs are boring, tedious, and unfulfilling. Who wouldn't rather not work? Parents know how hard it is to train their kids to overcome laziness. **"One who is slack in his work is brother to one who destroys"** (Proverbs 18:9).

Procrastination. This is the college-educated version of laziness in that the person pretends to have a plan to get things done, just not now. Unfortunately tomorrow will bring new excuses to put things off. **"Sluggards do not plow in season; so at harvest time they look but find nothing"** (Proverbs 20:4).

Blaming. With a small amount of effort, you can blame your unhappy life situation on other people—your dysfunctional spouse, your ex-spouse, your father, your mother, your expensive children. Some people even want to blame God: **"A person's own folly leads to their ruin, yet their heart rages against the Lord"** (Proverbs 19:3).

Entitlement. Somebody else owes me. I have a right to a decent income. (*Psst*—actually no, you don't.)

Ignorance. Financial literacy takes as much work to learn as reading or math literacy. It's hard work, takes time, and sometimes needs some pain to help the learning process. Financially literate parents are a great blessing and need to be heeded: **"My son, do not forget my teaching, but keep my commands in your heart, for they will prolong your life many years and bring you prosperity"** (Proverbs 3:1,2).

> **Financial literacy takes as much work to learn as reading or math literacy.**

Missing one or both parents. Know what's worse than having parents who aren't good money managers? Not having a father or mother at all.

A parent is a fountain of life wisdom, and even when they are not good at something, the children can learn how not to do certain things. And even if the parents' financial track record isn't that hot, they probably know what they did wrong and can counsel the kids not to repeat their mistakes. God's original plan was to have a mature adult male and female present every day for the spiritual and intellectual formation of children: **"Listen, my son, to your father's instruction and do not forsake your mother's teaching"** (Proverbs 1:8).

No ambition. Some children just aren't motivated to improve themselves. They loaf through their education years and neglect their chances to prepare for adult life. They become adults who aren't motivated to improve themselves. That inertia sometimes masquerades as prudence, unwilling to take any risk or try something new: **"There's a lion in the road, a fierce lion roaming the streets!"** (Proverbs 26:13).

Work

There are only a few ways to acquire money, property, and financial security:

- *Gifts* (a little hard to control or predict)

- *Inheriting* (also a little hard to control or predict); even if your parents are well-off now, their nursing home and medical costs in their elder years might eat up all their assets.

- *Investing* (see pages 39–40)

- *Gambling.* It's more likely that you will lose money than make anything (see pages 46–47).

- *Exchanging.* Barter is less common than four thousand years ago, but it still happens.

- *Stealing* and other illegal/immoral ways to get what belongs to others (see pages 41–43)

- *Work*

It is that seventh way that will do the most to provide for you and your family. God loves work. He invented it, and he is immersed in it himself. Jesus told his friends and his enemies, **"My Father is always at his work to this very day, and I too am working"** (John 5:17). Some people think of heaven as eight million billion years of being on vacation, but I rather think that our heavenly experience will be fruitful and productive effort. I expect to be working, and enjoying it, in heaven.

We pray often for daily bread. Occasionally God

decides that a miracle is needed, but most of the time he answers that prayer by giving us personal talents and then work opportunities. The book of Proverbs enthusiastically recommends hard work and has only withering comments for the lazy and sluggish. In one of Proverbs' most well-known poetic stretches, the writer chooses one particular animal as a role model for our work lives:

The book of Proverbs enthusiastically recommends hard work.

"Go to the ant, you sluggard; consider its ways and be wise! It has no commander, no overseer or ruler, yet it stores its provisions in summer and gathers its food at harvest. How long will you lie there, you sluggard? When will you get up from your sleep? A little sleep, a little slumber, a little folding of the hands to rest—and poverty will come on you like a thief and scarcity like an armed man" (6:6-11).

Idleness, fooling around, wasting time, and laziness are all compelling behaviors. Even as a senior citizen I feel their pull. I have a "Demotivation" poster of a young man gazing dreamily into the sky with the legend, "Hard work often pays off after time, but laziness always pays off now." Every parent who has had to light a fire underneath kids to get them moving in a productive direction knows the power of idleness philosophy.

We have to believe that there will be a payoff that will more than justify the exertion. Proverbs helps with that motivation: **"The appetite of laborers works for them; their hunger drives them on"** (Proverbs 16:26). **"Lazy hands make for poverty, but diligent hands bring wealth"** (Proverbs 10:4). **"Those who work their land will have abundant food, but those who chase fantasies have no sense"** (Proverbs 12:11). **"A sluggard's appetite is never filled, but the desires of the diligent are fully satisfied"** (Proverbs 13:4). **"All hard work brings a profit, but mere talk leads only to poverty"** (Proverbs 14:23).

God will not lie to you. He's right about work.

Spending

There are few healthy financial habits more important than these: Live within your means. Choose to spend less than you take in. Work on your self-discipline and self-control. Find the joy of living small, deferring today's pleasures for tomorrow's greater prosperity. **"Better a little with the fear of the Lord than great wealth with turmoil. Better a small serving of vegetables with love than a fattened calf with hatred"** (Proverbs 15:16,17). Respect the greed and gluttony and appetites and insecurities and covetousness that lurk in your heart, and give them no oxygen. **"Like a city whose walls are broken through is a person who lacks self-control"** (Proverbs 25:28).

Retailers and marketers are experts in human behavior. They search endlessly for the emotional triggers that will get you to spend money. They are wizards at designing seductive "point-of-purchase" displays to lure you into buying more than you planned. They train their salespeople to "upsell," always looking to get their hands deeper into your purse or wallet. Our world has always been awash in advertising, but it is a special challenge to stay financially sane in this completely mad digital age. Now that you can go shopping at home with just a few screen taps on your mobile device, the assault of advertising has found new ways to get into your head.

Never underestimate your appetites. **"Whoever**

loves pleasure will become poor" (Proverbs 21:17). "Do not join those who drink too much wine or gorge themselves on meat, for drunkards and gluttons become poor, and drowsiness clothes them in rags" (Proverbs 23:20,21).

Or this: "When you sit to dine with a ruler, note well what is before you, and put a knife to your throat if you are given to gluttony. Do not crave his delicacies, for that food is deceptive" (Proverbs 23:1-3).

How Much Is Enough?

Among the most maddening financial questions of all: How much is enough? How do I know how big to set my goals? How do I know if my life has been a success? How big a financial reserve do I need? How will I know the right time to retire?

While it's good to have numerical goals and targets, it is not good to think, "I'll be happy when I'm financially secure." You may never think you're secure and thus never give yourself permission to feel happy and contented. God's wonderful promises of daily forgiveness and providing mean you can choose to be happy *right now*. Even when you're in the very early stages of a long financial journey, even when you're living small and humbly, you can choose to praise God for all he's given you *right now*.

If you look for evidences of God's steady blessings, you will find them.

"**Godliness with contentment is great gain. For we brought nothing into the world, and we can take nothing out of it. But if we have food and clothing, we will be content with that**" (1 Timothy 6:6–8).

Contentment is learned behavior. It is a conscious choice in response to God's gifts. If you look for financial dangers and risks and setbacks, you will always find them. But if you look for evidences of God's steady blessings, you will find them too. "**That each of them may eat and drink,** and find satisfaction in all their toil—this is the gift of God" (Ecclesiastes 3:13). **"When God gives someone wealth and possessions, and the ability to enjoy them, to accept their lot and be happy in their toil—this is a gift of God"** (Ecclesiastes 5:19).

There is a mysterious set of verses near the end of Proverbs, penned by a completely unknown biblical author named Agur. This man crafted an unusual prayer, asking God's help in keeping him between the twin pits of despair and pride:

"Two things I ask of you, Lord; do not refuse me before I die: Keep falsehood and lies far from me; give me neither poverty nor riches, but give me only my daily bread. Otherwise, I may have too much and disown you and say, 'Who is the Lord?' Or I may become poor and steal, and so dishonor the name of my God" (Proverbs 30:7–9).

Say it with me: "I love my life."

Debt

A friend of mine was telling me about her mother's financial advice. When she was just starting out in her professional career, her mother told her to get some credit cards and then just go shopping and load 'em up. "You only have to pay the minimum each month!" her mother crowed. In her mother's mind, this setup was a miraculous deal just too good to pass up, and she excitedly shared it with her daughter. Alas, dear mother. She had no conception of consumer debt and its loan-shark interest rates.

We are a debt-loving nation, and I am nervous that the young are so used to it that they don't fear it enough. It is not possible to get exact figures about the debt load of the average American family (different financial writers will quote statistics that vary somewhat), but the average American household with credit cards carries unpaid balances of around $16,000; the average new car loan on a purchase is $29,000; the average home mortgage is around $180,000; and the average college graduate emerges from school with $37,000 in student loan debt. Over 10% of those student loans are at risk of default.

King Solomon wrote this almost three thousand years ago: **"The rich rule over the poor, and the borrower is slave to the lender"** (Proverbs 22:7). Nothing much has changed in three millennia. At least when you get a loan through a bank, credit union, or other financial institution, the institution will do its underwriting and be the grown-up in the room. You have to demonstrate ability to repay, and in the case of a house or car, there is some collateral. The terrible danger of incurring credit card or student loan debt is that they have no collateral, and thus have a much higher interest rate, and there is no bank "grown-up" to say no to you when you have the impulse to borrow.

Credit card loans are especially brutal. The average interest cost on unpaid balances is 16%—which means half of all cards charge even *more* than that. Those cards are like financial opioids—they seem like a quick solution to a problem, but if you can't pay them off within 30 days, the interest begins to compound rapidly. With all loans, but especially your credit cards, **"let no debt remain outstanding"** (Romans 13:8).

The same is true of borrowing from friends or family. It is so easy to take advantage of people you know—what are they going to do if you don't meet your agreed-on payment schedule? Sue you? Have you arrested? But the Christian way is to treat these debts with utmost seriousness: **"Do not say to your neighbor, 'Come back tomorrow and I'll give it to you'—when you already have it with you"** (Proverbs 3:28).

Here are three tips I've received from people smarter than I:

1. Be careful how much college you buy. And—

be careful of how much room and board you have to buy along with it. Could you attend college in town and live at home? Does attending a low-cost community junior college for two years get the cost down? Plan out for ten years what your payment schedule will be. How big a bite will that take out of your hoped-for salary after graduation?

2. Shop around for loans. Don't get rushed. Even a 1% difference will make a huge difference over the years.

3. Develop a relationship with a financial advisor whom you can trust. Run your borrowing and debt-servicing plans through him or her.

Generosity

Of all the learned behaviors about money, generosity probably comes last and is the hardest. The reformer Martin Luther said that the last part of a sinner to be converted is the wallet. The other money lessons at least are disciplines that lead to one's prosperity. Giving money away means you'll have less of it, right? Well, er, no. In God's divine convection system, generosity only taps you into the circular flow of resources, and God will more than replenish anything you may give to him or to other people.

Our financial gifts to our congregations and ministries that we care about are thank offerings of love for all that God has done for us. They aren't taxes or dues. They aren't mandatory tithes as commanded in the Old Testament. They are voluntary gifts of love to a God who has given us so much, and in fact were really never even ours in the first place. We're just giving God what belongs to him anyway.

All are appropriate. Sometimes the gifts are extravagant, which is only what he deserves, as was the extremely expensive perfume with which Jesus was anointed in Bethany (Matthew 26:6–13). Sometimes the gifts may seem pitifully small, as were the pennies given by a widow (Luke 21:1,2). What matters is that the giver is honoring the Giver, grateful for grace, happy that he or she can show this personal devotion.

Here are the great principles of Christian generosity:

Everybody
"No one is to appear before me empty-handed" (Exodus 23:15).

God's portion first
"Honor the LORD with your wealth, with the *firstfruits* of all your crops; then your barns will be filled to overflowing, and your vats will brim over with new wine" (Proverbs 3:9,10).

Joyful
"Each of you should give what you have decided in your heart to give, not reluctantly or under compulsion, for God loves a cheerful giver" (2 Corinthians 9:7).

Proportionate
"Now about the collection for the Lord's people: Do what I told the Galatian churches to do. On the first day of every week, each one of you should set aside a sum of money in keeping with your income" (1 Corinthians 16:1,2).

Trusting
"You will be enriched in every way so that you can be generous on every occasion, and through us your generosity will result in thanksgiving to God" (2 Corinthians 9:11).

Leaders go first

"'Who is willing to consecrate themselves to the Lᴏʀᴅ today?' Then the leaders of families, the officers of the tribes of Israel, the commanders of thousands and commanders of hundreds, and the officials in charge of the king's work gave willingly. They gave toward the work on the temple of God five thousand talents and ten thousand darics of gold, ten thousand talents of silver, eighteen thousand talents of bronze and a hundred thousand talents of iron" (1 Chronicles 29:5-7).

God's blessings to his believing children are not intended to stop with his children. He shows mercy to them, intending that they will show mercy to others. He forgives them with the intent that they let go of their bitterness and grudges toward each other. He is generous with us with the intent that we would be kind and generous with those in need around us.

- "Do not withhold good from those to whom it is due, when it is in your power to act" (Proverbs 3:27).

- "One person gives freely, yet gains even more; another withholds unduly, but comes to poverty. A generous person will prosper; whoever refreshes others will be refreshed" (Proverbs 11:24,25).

- "Whoever is kind to the poor lends to the LORD, and he will reward them for what they have done" (Proverbs 19:17).

- "Those who give to the poor will lack nothing, but those who close their eyes to them receive many curses" (Proverbs 28:27).

Saving and Investing

Americans used to be savers. Perhaps the generation of people who had survived the Depression and WWII learned to be self-sufficient. The national rate of saving in the 1950s–1980s was 10+%. It peaked at 17% in 1975, and then began a steep plunge, bottoming out at a measly 1.9% in 2005. What happened? Did the children and grandchildren of the Depression survivors forget the painful lessons of the past? The savings rate has perked up a little and gotten over 4%, but that is still inadequate, according to any financial advisor you'd consult. They would implore you to have the discipline to save at least 10% of your take-home pay. These days 40% of Americans have no savings, retirement or otherwise (some say the number is 50+%). They live paycheck to paycheck.

The Bible has some sharp remarks about the practice of consuming everything you make: **"The wise store up choice food and olive oil, but fools gulp theirs down"** (Proverbs 21:20). Having a clear saving strategy that you set up when you're young and stick to your whole working life is now more important than ever. The days of "defined benefits" pensions are over, at least in private industry. Financial advisors will tell you that you should build up savings of ten times your last annual salary before you retire. So how are you doing?

Other than inheriting a pile from a rich uncle or receiving a huge gift out of nowhere, the only way you can build assets like that are by patient and disciplined saving and investing. **"Whoever gathers money little by little makes it grow"** (Proverbs 13:11). The miracle of compounding means that the younger you are when you start, the bigger the result when you want to retire.

Another principle that all advisors will recommend is to have a diverse array of investments. Solomon encouraged that strategy long ago: **"Sow your seed in the morning, and at evening let your hands not be idle, for you do not know which will succeed, whether this or that, or whether both will do equally well"** (Ecclesiastes 11:6).

Jesus himself, though his earthly net worth was probably pretty small, understood that money as cash was daily losing its value through inflation, that money placed in a savings account would at least have a small yield, but that being fully invested in business was the best strategy. The nobleman in his parable showed these timeless principles: **"He called ten of his servants and gave them ten minas. 'Put this money to work,' he said, 'until I come back.' . . . 'Why then didn't you** [at least] **put my money on deposit, so that when I came back, I could have collected it with interest?'"** (Luke 19:13,23).

Cheating

"There's a sucker born every minute." P.T. Barnum, showbiz promoter extraordinaire, supposedly said that. People have been hustling and swindling and extorting and scamming and cheating one another since the days of Adam and Eve. When the Spirit of the Lord takes up residence in your heart, however, there will be none of that in your life. Your relationship with your employer is a sacred trust. Your customers' well-being is equally untouchable. If you love your neighbor as yourself, you will respect his or her property as though it were your own.

If you love your neighbor as yourself, you will respect his or her property as though it were your own.

Cheaters sometimes self-soothe their guilty hearts by saying things like, "The money makes it all right." Well, money never makes evil all right. You may have gotten money through cheating, but your soul is now sicker, your conscience is protesting, and the eyes of your God were on you the whole time. **"Ill-gotten treasures have no lasting value"** (Proverbs 10:2). **"The Lord detests dishonest scales, but accurate weights find favor with him"** (Proverbs 11:1). **"A kindhearted woman gains honor, but ruthless men gain only wealth. Those who are kind benefit themselves,** but the cruel bring ruin on themselves. A wicked person earns deceptive wages, but the one who sows righteousness reaps a sure reward" (Proverbs 11:16–18).

Scripture has much to say about financial cheating. Why is that? Is it possibly because Satan uses money hunger to corrupt the hearts of even the children of God? Do you believe this: **"Dishonest money dwindles away"** (Proverbs 13:11). Or this? **"Food gained by fraud tastes sweet, but one ends up with a mouth full of gravel"** (Proverbs 20:17). Or this? **A fortune made by a lying tongue is a fleeting vapor and a deadly snare"** (Proverbs 21:6).

There have always been rackets that twist laws and the legal system: **"The wicked accept bribes in secret to pervert the course of justice"** (Proverbs 17:23). Real estate fraud is nothing new: **"Do not move an ancient boundary stone set up by your ancestors"** (Proverbs 22:28). It's never been too hard to cheat the poor because the rich have way better lawyers. But don't do it, because the poor have an even better Attorney—**"Do not exploit the poor because they are poor and do not crush the needy in court, for the Lord will take up their case and will exact life for life"** (Proverbs 22:22,23).

The Word has still more to say to our world: **"Whoever robs their father or mother and says, 'It's not wrong,' is partner to one who destroys"** (Proverbs 28:24). **"Extortion turns a** wise person into a fool, and a bribe corrupts the heart" (Ecclesiastes 7:7). **"Better a little with righteousness than much gain with injustice"** (Proverbs 16:8).

One of Jesus' gospel triumphs was in the life of a tax collector named Zacchaeus. Though small in stature, he had grown big in wealth by chiseling and squeezing his fellow Israelites at his tax office. The mercy that God showed him transformed his worldview, and he resolved publicly to mend his ways and make full restitution: **"Here and now I give half of my possessions to the poor, and if I have cheated anybody out of anything, I will pay back four times the amount"** (Luke 19:8).

Is there anything in *your* past financial dealings that you need to fix?

Lending

Lending has its own risks. William Shakespeare had his character Polonius give this advice to his impetuous son Laertes in *Hamlet*: "Neither a borrower nor a lender be, for loan oft loses both itself and friend, and borrowing dulls the edge of husbandry (i.e., the willingness to work hard)." Still pretty good advice. If you choose to lend money within your family or to a friend, you might just consider in advance what you would do if the money didn't get repaid on time. Would that ruin a relationship? You might be better off just deciding on an amount to give the person.

The Bible doesn't talk a lot about lending. In Bible times, as in our times, there were commercial loans available as well as borrowing between friends and family members. In Exodus 22:25-27, Moses counseled the Israelites not to take advantage of the poor in their lending practices. In Luke 6:32-36, Jesus urged his disciples to show financial generosity and compassion to people who were struggling.

Jesus also blasted the religious leaders of his time for making money off their investments in banks but for having no heart for vulnerable people caught up in emergencies: **"Watch out for the teachers of the law. They like to walk around in flowing robes and be greeted with respect in the marketplaces, and have the most important seats in the synagogues and the places of honor** at banquets. They devour widows' houses and for a show make lengthy prayers. These men will be punished most severely" (Mark 12:38-40).

A common practice in Bible times was cosigning for loans. It was an easy way to look like a power broker and to swagger in front of friends by offering to guarantee loans. Solomon counseled that it's such a poor idea that you should run in the opposite direction:

"My son, if you have put up security for your neighbor, if you have shaken hands in pledge for a stranger, you have been trapped by what you said, ensnared by the words of your mouth. So do this, my son, to free yourself, since you have fallen into your neighbor's hands: Go—to the point of exhaustion—and give your neighbor no rest! Allow no sleep to your eyes, no slumber to your eyelids. Free yourself, like a gazelle from the hand of the hunter, like a bird from the snare of the fowler" (Proverbs 6:1-5).

Gambling

The Bible doesn't talk much about gambling either, although various games of chance were widespread from earliest history. Six-sided cubes with numbers on them have been found in archeological excavation sites in the Middle East and are estimated to have come from at least 2,500–3,000 B.C. Dice were everywhere in the Roman world, and the soldiers especially, like soldiers of every era, loved to gamble with them to ease the boredom of military life.

Gambling is everywhere today and easier than ever to get involved in. Most states have casinos, and most gas stations and food stores sell lottery tickets. Online poker attracts millions of players, as does sports betting. As if golf isn't challenging enough, a foursome will set up a "friendly' Nassau (wager) before their round to increase the ~~pressure~~ enjoyment. And of course Las Vegas, the dream vacation spot for many Americans, exists because of and for gambling. Even the Vegas airport is packed with slot machines.

God gives you the dignity and responsibility of making good choices with your money.

Gambling is often considered evil, a vice. Indeed, it has a long connection with organized crime. Gambling is also notoriously addictive—the fantasies of quick wealth stay in people's heads and sometimes lead to destructive compulsive behaviors. But the Bible doesn't call it a sin, and therefore we should be very careful about imposing guilt on people who choose to gamble. God gives you the dignity and responsibility of making good choices with your money. But here are some thoughts for Christians who wish to gamble:

1. Can you afford to lose everything you're gambling? Can you lose without bitterness? Can you stop? Is this truly just entertainment for you? Can you walk away without feeling as though you "have to get your money back"?

2. Are you stealing from other obligations to have money to gamble with? Is your family financially secure? Does your spouse know what you're doing, or are you hiding your activity from family?

3. Do you have to borrow money to gamble?

4. Are you stealing money from your offerings to God for your gambling activities?

5. Can the other people you're gambling with pass the above four tests?

6. Is your desire to hit it big by gambling destroying your patience with building wealth day by day, paycheck by paycheck?

Taxes

It doesn't much matter what you think of your tax burden—it comes at you without any effort on your part. Federal and state income taxes are withheld from your paycheck; you are on the hook for income from dividends, interest, and capital gains; you are invoiced for your city and county property taxes (or pay it through your rent checks); and every nonfood purchase you make takes a cut for the state through the sales tax.

A lot of money is subtracted from people through taxation. One way to grasp the impact is to note "Tax Freedom Day," i.e., the day in April or May that marks when you've finally made enough money to satisfy your tax obligations. The midpoint of personal taxation is about 31%—that is, roughly a third of what the average Joe and Jane make goes to taxes.

I haven't run into too many people who think their tax burden is too light. Honestly, I have done my own share of tax grumbling. Our country's independence movement originated from a tax revolt, did it not? The Jewish people at Jesus' time hated the Romans' tax system and its rapacious network of tax collectors, who were backed up by the occupying Roman army. People like Zacchaeus and Levi were resented and shunned as collaborators and chiselers. They occupied the same social level as the town prostitutes.

And yet Jesus counseled his followers to submit

to their governments, just and unjust, and pay what they owed. **"After Jesus and his disciples arrived in Capernaum, the collectors of the two-drachma temple tax came to Peter and asked, 'Doesn't your teacher pay the temple tax?' 'Yes, he does,' he replied"** (Matthew 17:24,25). Jesus then miraculously provided a tetradrachma and instructed Peter to make the payment.

Another time Jesus was challenged by his enemies with what they thought was the perfect trick question: **"'Tell us then, what is your opinion? Is it right to pay the imperial tax to Caesar or not?' But Jesus, knowing their evil intent, said, 'You hypocrites, why are you trying to trap me? Show me the coin used for paying the tax.' They brought him a denarius, and he asked them, 'Whose image is this? And whose inscription?' 'Caesar's,' they replied. Then he said to them, 'So give back to Caesar what is Caesar's, and to God what is God's'"** (Matthew 22:17–21).

We don't put the faces of living presidents on our money, but the name of our country is prominently displayed on every coin and bill. In addition, we have the stupendous blessing of living in an era, and living in a particular country, that allows a great deal of citizen input into how we are governed. It is the people we have elected that have set our levels of taxation. And while tax evasion is a crime, tax minimization is not—get good professional advice on how you can pay your fair share but not more than your fair share.

St. Paul lived under a much greater tyranny. The Emperor Nero would one day approve of his martyrdom and launch a major persecution of Christians. And had not the Roman governor of Judea and Samaria ordered the execution of his Lord and Savior? And yet he said this about the people's tax obligations: **"This is also why you pay taxes, for the authorities are God's servants, who give their full time to governing. Give to everyone what you owe them: If you owe taxes, pay taxes; if revenue, then revenue; if respect, then respect; if honor, then honor"** (Romans 13:6,7).

I promise to be more cheerful at tax time. Will you join me?

Your Financial Legacy

Some people don't like going to hospitals to visit friends or family because, as they would say, they don't like being around all that sickness and suffering. Maybe they're afraid of what lies ahead for them. Some shun funeral homes for the same reason—the thought of death creeps them out.

That same fear and avoidance mentality might be what keeps so many of us from preparing a last will and testament. Only about 44% of American adults currently have a legal will. Arrgh! Arranging our financial affairs so that our exit from the stage won't cause family turmoil is an important part of money wisdom. It is our last great piece of work as God's stewards of his treasures. If you die intestate, the state will make the decisions on disposal of your property, and not a dime of it will be directed to any ministries or charities no matter how much the deceased loved and supported them in life.

It is a great service that we seniors can perform for the young ones coming up that we don't consume everything we've accumulated but leave a stake for them. King Solomon had some experience with a recurring sad situation: **"I have seen a grievous evil under the sun: wealth hoarded to the harm of its owners, or wealth lost through some misfortune, so that when they have children there is nothing left for them to inherit"** (Ecclesiastes 5:13,14).

Another good reason to do careful estate planning is that you don't want to ruin your children and grandchildren by giving them too much. People tend not to respect fully money that they didn't have to work for. Again, nothing new here: **"An inheritance claimed too soon will not be blessed at the end"** (Proverbs 20:21). Easy come, easy go.

We don't have to dread end-of-life decisions *because our lives don't end* when we die. We just transition into the glorious life of heaven. It can be a *pleasure* to lay good plans for the disposition of our assets. **"A good person leaves an inheritance for their children's children"** (Proverbs 13:22). And only if we have specified our church or charitable agencies in the legal document can any legacies be given to them.

We don't have to dread end-of-life decisions because our lives don't end when we die.

Conclusion

If you are well along in years, you have undoubtedly learned a lot of money lessons along your path and recognized the truths in these Scripture passages. If you are young, this may all seem overwhelming. Fear not. It took me decades to acquire these insights, and I'm still learning. Just as it's good to review your financial plan every couple of years, it would probably be a good idea to review these scriptural principles and recommit to them. I hope this book can also provide a framework for you to use in mentoring the young people in your life.

I have made financial mistakes, and you will too. Those mistakes are failures only if you don't learn from them. What I can absolutely guarantee to you is that the more you align your money thinking with God's Word, the happier you will be, the more contented and satisfied with your life, and the more confident you will be.

And it sure makes for a happier home.

About the Writer

Pastor Mark Jeske brings the good news of Jesus Christ to viewers of *Time of Grace* in weekly 30-minute programs broadcast across America and around the world on local television, cable, and satellite, as well as on-demand streaming via the internet. He is the senior pastor at St. Marcus Church, a thriving multicultural congregation in Milwaukee, Wisconsin. Mark is the author of several books and dozens of devotional booklets on various topics. He and his wife, Carol, have four adult children.

About Time of Grace

Time of Grace is for people who want more growth and less struggle in their spiritual walk. The timeless truth of God's Word is delivered through television, print, and digital media with millions of content engagements each month. We connect people to God's grace so they know they are loved and forgiven and so they can start living in the freedom they've always wanted.

To discover more, please visit timeofgrace.org, download our free app at timeofgrace.org/app, or call 800.661.3311.

Help share God's message of grace!

Your generosity and prayer support take the gospel of grace to others through our ministry outreach and help them find the restart with Jesus they need.

Give today at timeofgrace.org/give or by calling 800.661.3311.

Thank you!